# Biggest, Smallest, Fastest, Slowest

### Stanford Makishi

## Contents

**Rigby**

A Harcourt Achieve Imprint

www.Rigby.com
1-800-531-5015

# The Biggest
## Animal on Land

The biggest animal on land is the **African elephant.**

This elephant can be 25 feet long.

It can weigh 14,000 pounds.

That's as much as a school bus!

# The Biggest
# Animal in the Sea

The **blue whale** is the biggest animal in the sea.

It is more than 100 feet long.

That is as long as 4 African elephants!

One blue whale can weigh more than 20 school buses!

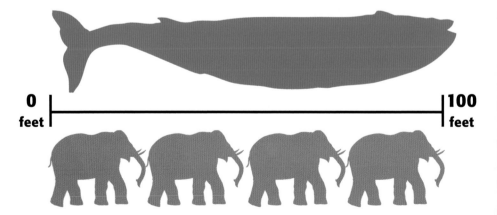

0 feet | 100 feet

# The Smallest
## Animal on Land

The smallest mammal on land is
the **bumblebee bat**.
This bat's body is only as big
as a dime!
It lives in a cave.

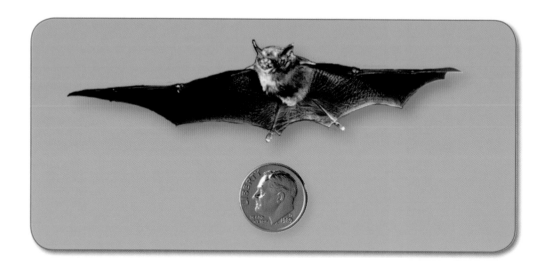

# The Smallest
# Fish in the Sea

The smallest fish in the sea is
the **stout infant fish**.

This fish is smaller than your
thumbnail!

This tiny fish lives in the sea
near Australia.

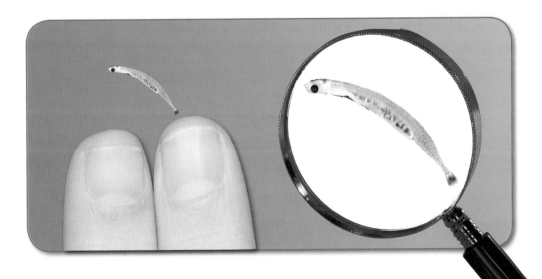

# The Fastest
## Animal on Land

The fastest animal on land is
the **cheetah**.

It can run more than 60 miles
an hour!

A cheetah eats meat.

A cheetah's speed helps
it catch its food.

# The Fastest
# Fish in the Sea

The **sailfish** is the fastest fish
in the sea.
It speeds along at more than
60 miles an hour!
That's as fast as a car.
Its fin looks like
a big sail.

# The Slowest
## Animal on Land

The slowest animal on land is
the **three-toed sloth**.

This sloth lives in the jungle.

It moves from branch to branch
very slowly.

A sloth only moves 10 feet every
minute when in the trees.

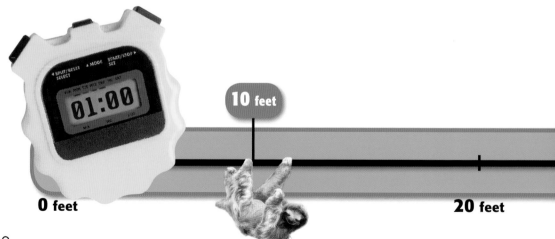

10 feet

01:00

0 feet

20 feet

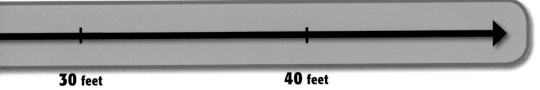

**30 feet**          **40 feet**

13

# The Slowest Fish in the Sea

The **sea horse** is the slowest fish in the sea.

Sea horses don't go far.

In one minute, a sea horse only swims about one foot!

It stops often and holds on to things with its tail.

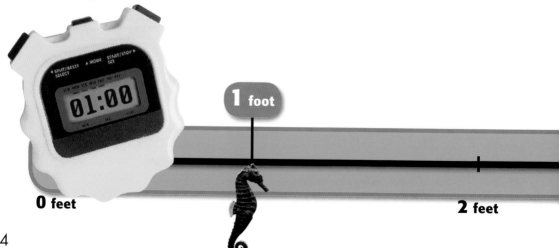

01:00

**1 foot**

**0 feet**

**2 feet**

**3 feet**          **4 feet**

# Glossary

African elephant

blue whale

bumblebee bat

cheetah

sailfish

sea horse

stout infant fish

three-toed sloth